W9-CIK-201

# EVERYTHING

Also by Andrea Cohen

*Nightshade*

*Unfathoming*

*Furs Not Mine*

*Kentucky Derby*

*Long Division*

*The Cartographer's Vacation*

# EVERYTHING

# Andrea Cohen

Four Way Books
Tribeca

*Every toy has the right to break.*

—Antonio Porchia

*for Razia*

Copyright © 2021 by Andrea Cohen
No part of this book may be used or reproduced in any manner without written
permission except in the case of brief quotations embodied in critical articles and reviews.

Library of Congress Cataloging-in-Publication Data

Names: Cohen, Andrea, 1961- author.
Title: Everything / Andrea Cohen.
Description: New York : Four Way Books, [2021] |
Identifiers: LCCN 2020037832 | ISBN 9781945588686 (trade paperback)
Subjects: LCGFT: Poetry.
Classification: LCC PS3603.O3415 E94 2021 | DDC 811/.6--dc23
LC record available at https://lccn.loc.gov/2020037832

This book is manufactured in the United States of America and printed on
acid-free paper.

Four Way Books is a not-for-profit literary press. We are grateful for the assistance
we receive from individual donors, public arts agencies, and private foundations.

This publication is made possible with public funds from the
National Endowment for the Arts

and from the New York State Council on the Arts, a state agency,

We are a proud member of the Community of Literary Magazines and Presses.

Contents

I

II

III

IV

I

# Wrecking Ball

Its offices are thin
air. On days off

it still goes in—
wrecking balls are

workaholics. They
hang around up

there, and even
the idea of big

sky crumbles.

# Desert Isle

If I have to
go there, I'd

like a phone-
book I can

sit on, on
a chair—

I'd like
to believe

I'm a child
someone

comes back for.

# Everything

*Everything was beautiful and*
*nothing hurt*, Kurt Vonnegut said.

*Everything was beautiful*
*and nothing hurt*, the girl

slurred to the artist
at the tattoo parlor.

The word made
flesh isn't fictional.

It's beautiful.
It hurts.

# Le Danton

She told me the name
of the poet and the name

of the café where he wrote
on St. Germaine. *Go there,*

she said. *See him.*
So I went and saw him

that winter, sitting
outside in a black

coat and ochre scarf.
He looked like a bee

exiled from summer.
He was talking

to the packets
of sugar on

the table. *Tell
me everything,* he

was saying. I was
nineteen and had

my whole life
to know nothing.

# After

After the accident we had
the phrase *after the accident.*

Also this: *before the accident.*
We had a drawer marked

*before and after,* and after
and before happenings

we'd add atrocities and
incidents and the wild

asters someone before
and after keeps leaving.

# Half Measures

She lamented her half-
empty cup, how

big it was, how
much emptiness

she'd been given.

# Craft Talk

I paint
small birds,

so when
they fly

off, their
loss might

seem
like less.

# Fellow Traveler

She went everywhere
with an empty suitcase.

You never know when
you'll need to leave

swiftly with nothing.

# Right as Rain

Try saying that
as the giraffes—

neck and neck—
are slowing

for Noah.

# Epicenter

The statues were inconsolable.
Someone had taken

their heads, and they
couldn't—in the grim

light see—which
way they'd taken.

# Ring

To throw your hat
in is to make

yourself bare-
headed, ready,

by oils to be
anointed, or by ark-

hard rains, of an
instant, stricken.

# Self Portrait with Eraser

I drew the eraser
first because I knew

it better than I knew
myself and because

it had been around
the block before me

and because it would,
after having its way

with me, rub up against
everything I'd ever loved.

# No One

*after Ani Gjika*


*No one I love was taken*
*into the woods and shot,*

you said. You said
this in a meadow

of a dress and kept
on talking and all

I saw was a forest,
all I heard was one

clean shot and no
one—toward the dear

clearing—running.

# The Bars Insist

The bars insist
they don't belong

in prison. We're not
even bars, they say.

We're stripes pried
from a zebra's back.

No one listens—not
the guards and not

petitions. No one
listens until a number

comes along insisting
he's a man, and

without a crop or
saddle, on seven

stripes rides off.

# Bootstraps

So you pulled
them up. What

cobbler made
those shoes

and whose
hands, asking

nothing, gave
them to you?

# Bruise

You've seen
skies like that

before or after
storms—as if

thugs could beat
even the idea

of milk
money from them.

# Weep Holes

We build these
into the dream-

house, holes drilled
into window sills,

so rainy days
drain out. No

dream's complete
without looking

ahead, without
seeing ourselves

looking back
at whom—

dreaming—
we'd been.

# Too Long

Too long at the fair, the song
laments. No one sings

of hanging around too
long at the hospital.

Someone kept getting
stale coffee in paper

cups, someone kept
punching a vending

machine, as if another
hour might come out.

# Rail

By the time we'd built
the handrail, the hand

had vanished—
yet still there was

a sky to rail at.

# Dust

We funnel it between the stones.
What stones become is what

holds them together. A crushing
summer: white hydrangeas, in

dry winds, nod. In Adirondacks
we can't fix, in a twilight beyond

repair, we recline, and an orange
tanager—which you asked

someone to come back
as—lights and vanishes.

# Openings

Eternity has closed its doors—
good riddance! I didn't want

forever forever—just this
pear tree, branches

backlit and the fruits
I can't get to.

# Shiva

Evenings we sit in the living
room, together. Friday I take

my mother's slot (noon)
at the beauty salon. Ruth,

who for forty years washed
her hair, washes mine.

We're all in the desert
together. Your mother

liked the water cold,
Ruth says: news to me.

From a thousand
mouths, our dead assemble.

II

# No Moon, But

I knew it was
the beekeeper

who touched me,
not because she

tasted of honey,
but because she

was unafraid
of being stung.

# Alchemy

I don't want
gold per se. I

want change.
Take my bright

ingots—dim
them. Gaze

this way—
rearrange me.

# Bees

Of course they buzz.
They make honey

without equivocating
and think nothing

of dying to defend
the hive: why

live without
systems to

transfigure nectar?

# Gaucín

The swallows
got into

the house
and made

of everything
a cathedral.

# Another Gift

Here's something I
have two of, someone

said, which meant
much, and then

someone without
a word handed

me the one
thing she had—

and I could
barely, in my one

head, hold it.

# Domestic

A man stands accused
of shooting at the moon—

which was naked and
out at such an hour.

# Announcement

The peonies will
receive you now.

# Tattoo

If I had one, it
would be an orchid

blossom falling
along my throat,

one petal
torn, tumbling

onto torso,
another inked

inside your hand.

# Stretch

The stretch of sea
between two signs

that read: *end*
*of guarded beach*

is roughly the wing-
span of a flightless

man, which is to
say, the size

of an embrace,
which is what

rough waters
require.

# Registry

They asked for what
they'd need: one

cup and one plate,
one day whose stunt

double would be
night, and two miner's

lights, for when
each was lost

to the other.

# Allée

She agreed to live
together only after

we'd hung pictures
of places on all

the walls, so everywhere
you looked there was

a sidestreet or green
allée, a vanishing

point to move toward.

# Magician

Anyone can saw
a woman in half.

The hard part
is sitting with

both halves at
breakfast, asking

one to pass
the salt and

the other to
lick your wounds.

That's what
polyamory is—

loving all
the charlatans

you are.

# Love

It's an extreme
sport—like in-
door beekeeping.

# Even

*after Bill Knott*

*Even your neck's a petty
crime*, he said to anyone

running past the bullet-
proof room he wasn't.

# Three Rivers

*after Wang An-Shih*

Three rivers yet
to cross. I'm

late. My houseboy
will be closing

the gate—and
my wife, maybe,

opening our
door for him.

# One-Two

One train came through
our whistle-stop town.

Being two people, we
got on, and dreaming

out one window
went two places.

# Rabbit Hole

Never move, my swell
friend Alice says, and

you'll never feel pain.
But never moving

bruises too—everything
with *never* stings.

# Pain and Suffering

She recorded
the silence

between us—
played it

back—made
me listen.

# Advert

Antique oval mirror—
will add beauty

to any room in
which beauty has

been installed,
and will mirror

everything you
live without.

# Gift

I gave her
my emptiness.

She put it
in a locket.

# First Love

She was
always

leaving
the dark on.

# Dusk

There was, as we walked
the salt flats at dusk,

an invisible thread
between us—

and then I felt
her invisible scissors.

# Chair

*for Naomi Wallace*

Not there—
the easy

chair recalls
all of you

too easily.
Sit instead

in the folding
chair, which

forgets every-
thing, save

collapsing when
you vanish.

# Rooms

People move
out. They leave

empty rooms.
You choose

what to do—
move into

them, or let
the emptiness

move into you.

# Pebble

I placed a pebble
where you were—

so you'd know
where to come

back to and how
hard days are.

# Mirror

I'd have paid
anything

for one
with another

face in it.

# Transatlantic

I gave you
my last stamp—
send it back.

# The Last Word

You
can have it—

as long as I
can have

my silence.

# Matinee

*Performing love* is what
she said. It was the first

time I'd heard this
expression, and the first

time is special—
you want, at first,

to bow or curtsy,
to listen for applause,

for the mercy
of a curtain.

# Playing Field

You were standing
in the rain

with a yellow tulip
for someone else,

and leveled I
was—the house we

never built by
one gust flattened.

# Bridge

Where there was
one, now sky

and river. Now
me here and you—

where?—and a cherry
blossom that recalls

evenings walking
on water.

# Seaside

Before the day at the beach,
we scouted out the day

at the beach, because
nothing happens without

planning, because we had
to plant the sand and

the idea of happiness.
We had to haul in

the water. All our
pleasures were forays

into wilds, were carry
in and out—like

our bodies, which
glistened, and were gone.

# Punctuated

A moon moves
across the night—

bright period
whose dark

sentence keeps
getting longer.

What, standing by
that window, did

you not say?

# With

It's a four-
letter word

when you're
without.

# With Us

It was dark—
the blind blind-
folding the blind.

# Forced

When everywhere, doors
are closing, remember

the branch a lightning
storm gave you, how

you sat in a room,
beside someone, barely

touching, stick of forsythia
in jam jar of water.

Inside that storm, one
hundred suns opened.

# December, Brightening

I came home
late to the broken

porch light fixed—
handiwork of an old

love's new flame.

# Orchard

The apple trees
were growing

peaches, and
in the lemon

grove, persimmons.
I'd have saved

a plum
from the fig

tree—but
I dreamed you.

III

# Gratitude

*after Agnes Martin*

How fortunate, having
fallen, to fall in
with a ladder        .
made of light.
How inviting
ideas are: climbing
into bigger, into
better bright. I
tried and tried,
but couldn't, on
two rungs, hold
fast. Panicked, I
was, until recalling
the Alpinist slipped
inside a crevasse,
a man, who, frostbit,
exhausted, unable
to climb up, willed
himself to slip
down more. One
goes, sometimes,
that deep into an icy
self and finds therein
an eyelet of light, an

opening, and ghost-
like, from some
ancient glacier stumbles.

# In the Car with the Theoretical Physicist

It's hard to hear her—
not because she's
theoretical, but because
of the dark matter
between us, what takes
up space but won't
engage with light. My
jacket is black, she says,
tugging on it, because
it absorbs light. My
muffler is loud and our
being here together
or anywhere, highly
unlikely. Now she's
on a plane, now I'm
at a table in Madrid.
People are always
leaving. We could call
the five or six mass
extinctions mass
migrations, but still they
would be sad. Everything
moves too fast into the past
and future. It's hard to keep

up, hard to not try to disguise
my voice and call in to the radio
station when the special guest
is the theoretical physicist,
hard not to ask: What should
we do if we stumble
into a black hole?
Duck and cover? Roll
with it? I'll take my answer
with a stiff drink, I say,
and she laughs, which
may be the only response
adequate to all this falling.

# Shadowboxer's Complaint

Shadows don't
fight fair.

# Instrumental

The flute sounds like night,
the Syrian composer says.

What sounds like day?
Anything a child plays.

# Naming

*for Stav Haber*

There's a name
for the flower
that comes
after the first
rain and a name
for that rain,
but no short-
hand for saying
we waited
a last time
in the rain
for that flower.

# How Everything

Two by two
assumes so much—
that this giraffe
will dig the other,
that the he-
bedbug likes shes,
or will, in the pinch
of apocalypse, make
do. Maybe you've
been in similar
tight spots, torrents
filling portals, all
you love getting
cozy with its maker.
Maybe the aardvark
can't believe he gets
for forty days to call
in sick, his only job to
re-aardvark the garden.
Maybe the pissant
in steerage goes
on autopilot, so
no flood beyond
measure, no stench

of leaving the known
world to drown, no
sudden dove in blue
or Brueghel's boy
falling, doesn't—
to some piss-
ant, get handed.

# What Would Have Been His Nineteenth Birthday

The day arrives—
like a riderless horse.

# Stop-Time

We give the clocks
a drink, so they'll

have something else
to do with their hands.

# Hymnals and Revivals

Friday nights we meet
in the church basement.
We drink coffee and talk
about what went wrong.
There's Orpheus, who's
pawned his lyre, and Lot's
wife, licking the salt
wound she is. We call
her Edie. Everyone goes
by one name: Hugh, who,
eyeing the rearview veered
into a crowd; Angus, who
turned in his lifeguard's
chair and missed a girl
going under. Edie regrets
not being born a horse
with blinders. Orpheus says
he wishes Eurydice never
loved him, but he doesn't
mean it. Above us,
hymnals and revivals,
believers heaven-bent.
Look, if I could go
back, I'd be gone.

# Salad Days

The cab I was
in passed too
fast for me
to say whether
that place we
loved was renamed
the Fatted or
the Fated Calf.
Names change,
and appetites,
and things
end badly
for the calf
either way,
though every-
thing in the rear
view seems green.

# Home

A road ran
past our house. I
ran faster.

# Horizon

A line I
will not cross.

# Ubi

In Latin, that's
when and where.
In operating theatres in
Glasgow, it's an acronym
for unexplained beer injuries,
which can happen anywhere,
at any intersection of how
and when. When you asked
where should we run
into each other, I could only
think of clichés and collisions,
of train stations and outsized clocks,
of an actor named Harold Lloyd
playing a man named Harold Lloyd,
of the two of them dangling
in one body from a skyscraper
in *Safety Last*, hands grasping
those of a clock, a sort of
*mano a reloj* filmed not atop
one building, but many
of differing heights, giving
the illusion of a man climbing
higher and higher, which
is what a man has to do

before he can kiss the girl.
That was a silent comedy.
Tragedies have words: tell
me where, and with how
little anesthesia, tell me when.

# Eleven

It's the eleventh
hour on the eleventh
floor. We chose this
apartment (if not
this hour) for the light,
though my father could,
from any height, look
back. Below are oaks
and magnolias and tracks
on which freight and passenger
trains pass, and my father
knows the difference by
the blowing of their horns,
both of which he prefers,
he says, to that other one
he's hearing, by which he
means Gabriel's, disguised
as tinnitus. He's remembering also,
since it's fall, the shofar Herb
Karp blew for the new year—
a sorrowing sound, he
always said, especially if
you were a ram. That
day we moved him

from the split-
level to the eleventh
floor, we brought a few
photographs and chairs,
lamps to see the
dark with, spoons,
a cup. It was a kind
of sky burial. He
has his pocket comb.
He has his wristwatch
with the busted strap,
he has his wallet
with a dollar. He's getting
smaller and smaller, his vast
past vaster. Looking out
from the eleventh hour
is like looking from
a hole punched to make
a room into a camera
obscura. Anything can
be a camera. Anyone
might be in this aerie,
but today it's us, watching
on the compact TV what

he watched, rapt
at the Imperial Theatre
in 1936—Buster Crabbe
as Flash Gordon, trying
to stop the planet Mongo
from colliding with Earth.
*I forget how it ends,* my
father says, *but it ends.*
And then we're looking
from the small screen out
the sliding glass toward
dusk, where below us,
on fluted, Spanish roofs,
two men in straw hats
are ambling the inclines
of tiles without ropes
or harnesses, without
fear. One man is tossing
bottles of water to the other,
who's smoking a cigarette
and catching the bottles,
and I'm thinking danger
and OSHA and laborers
in the vineyard and my

father from his eleventh
hour says—*lucky devils.*

# Crystal Ball

The crystal ball
falling

on the stone
floor tells all.

# Wind 101

I took
notes—

the wind
took those.

# The Blue Chair

That's not
where it happened.
It happened
on the Bauhaus
cloud of couch—
low to the ground, so
anyone could fall
onto it, with industrial
thick plastic on one
end, so anyone could
keep their shoes on,
could imagine they
might (if needed) leave
in a hurry. My father
was in the blue
chair. There was
an ottoman too. He
may have put his
feet up. He may
(he did, he
confessed) nod
off once or twice,
but mostly he
was a flight

controller there, making
sure his patients flying
into themselves didn't
crash too hard. Before
he died, I found
notes they wrote, hand-
written or typed bits
that said, *Doc, I'm
in a bad way,* or, *Doc,
you rule.* Even the auto
mechanic called him
Doc. He helped people
in ways I can't
say except to say I've
sat in a room
similar to those
offices and flown
lurchingly into
the past—and
as treacherous, into
what might be. Sunday
we'll stand by his
grave and say
grave things. Maybe

we're all nearly sound-
proof rooms and someone,
if we're lucky, stands
at the heaviness
of our doors, meaning
to listen.

# Tool Shed

I went there
after everything
and there
was a hand-
saw and a hammer,
drills and extra
drill bits, a spirit
level, tar and
pitch, wrenches
and screws—
evidence
that many
had come
before me
and from
some shattered
day made
a new
roof rise.

IV

# Either/Or

Would you rather be
Cain or Abel, my brother

asks. It's a trick question.
To say Cain is to raise

my hand against him,
to say Abel might spell

my death. It's a lesson
in lesser evils. I tell him:

I have no brother.

# Bomb Shelter

We had to keep
building them,

bigger and deeper,
because of how

many bombs
there were and

how afraid each
one was that

one of us
would set it off.

# 17th Century German Cobbler

He's seen
into the future

and given
up on boots.

# Guide to Becoming a Human Shield

Live
near
spears.

# Bible Study

How does a five-
year-old learn

to play dead?
Under what

sun can she
unlearn it?

# The Thing You

The thing you
can kill with

one hand you
can't—with

a thousand
hands—

bring back.

# Safety Glasses

The rose tint
isn't optional.

# Before the Headlines

The peony hears
the words—*flowering*

*bullets*—and over-
night goes white.

# Protocol

The prime minister
of Japan will

visit Pearl Harbor,
and in the manner of

the U.S. President
visiting Nagasaki,

not apologize.

# Bearer

We raised
the flag

from half
to full

mast—and
someone had

to ask: What
didn't happen?

# Peacekeepers

We're able
to contain it.

# Witness

I saw all
who saw
nothing.

# Another Mirror

He breaks the mirror
into spears, so no

one—nearing—
sees what he's seen.

# Tragic News

The tragedy was
that it was

usual and was
not news.

# Diaspora

I carry
everything

my people
lost.

# After the End

Listen, there were other
ends, other reckonings.

There were other one-
size boots, one kick

fits all. There were
other dark days no

night could mirror.
Hear me out—

if someone
above the rubble can.

# Swing State

Everyone insists
a pendulum swings—

it does, but it
hurts when

it hits you.

# Beating a Dead Horse

It still hurts
the girl whose
horse it was.

# No Man's Land

The soldier is burying
the boy with rocks

in his pocket
alive—on what

hilltop did
that soldier die?

# New Year

The wake-up
call of shofars

jars none
as much

as the ram
that got away.

# Bell

There was a bell
that rang

in my dreams.
It was beautiful

and I
was careful

not to ring it
too loudly—

lest I wake.

## Acknowledgments

I am grateful to the editors of these journals, in which the following poems appeared, sometimes in slightly different incarnations.

*Agni Online*: "Everything," "Pain and Suffering," "After"
*The Arkansas International*: "First Love"
*The Atlantic Monthly*: "Ring"
*The Cincinnati Review*: "Bridge," "Rail," "Futile"
*Construction*: "After the End," "Swing State"
*Diode*: "Winter," "No Moon, But," "Wind 101," "Openings," "Gift"
*Great River Review*: "Weep Holes," "Self Portrait with Eraser"
*The Kenyon Review*: "Transatlantic," "Dust," "Gaucín"
*The Literary Review*: "Allée," "Rooms"
*The New Yorker*: "Road Trip," "Wrecking Ball," "Registry," "Shiva"
*The New York Review of Books*: "Eleven"
*Plume*: "Hymnals and Revivals," "How Everything," "Figure of Speech"
*Post Road*: "Rabbit Hole," "Pebble," "Bootstraps," "Jehova," "Chair"
*Provincetown Arts*: "Gratitude"
*REI Force of Nature*: "No Moon, But"
*Spoon River Review*: "Forced," "Summons," "Bees,"
*Tikkun*: "Bible Study," "Gift"
*Resistance, Rebellion, Life: 50 Poems Now* (Knopf, 2017): "After the End"
*The Threepenny Review*: "In the Car with the Theoretical Physicist," "Ubi"

Thank you (for everything): Francesca Bewer, Amy Anderson, Gail Mazur, Robert Pinsky, Giavanna Munafo, Alice Sebold, Andy Senchak, Kiel Moe, Sarah Harwell, Tom Sleigh, Bruce Cohen, the Allenbergs (Andrea, Doug, Amanda, Simon), Naomi Wallace, Bosco, and Daisy. And my thanks to everyone at MacDowell and Four Way Books.

Andrea Cohen's poems and stories have appeared in *The New Yorker, The Atlantic Monthly, Poetry, The Threepenny Review, Glimmertrain, The New Republic, The Hudson Review* and elsewhere. Her earlier poetry collections include *Nightshade, Unfathoming, Furs Not Mine, Kentucky Derby, Long Division,* and *The Cartographer's Vacation.* She directs the Blacksmith House Poetry Series in Cambridge, MA.

Publication of this book was made possible by grants and donations. We are also grateful to those individuals who participated in our 2020 Build a Book Program. They are:

Anonymous (14), Robert Abrams, Nancy Allen, Maggie Anderson, Sally Ball, Matt Bell, Laurel Blossom, Adam Bohannon, Lee Briccetti, Therese Broderick, Jane Martha Brox, Christopher Bursk, Liam Callanan, Anthony Cappo, Carla & Steven Carlson, Paul & Brandy Carlson, Renee Carlson, Cyrus Cassells, Robin Rosen Chang, Jaye Chen, Edward W. Clark, Andrea Cohen, Ellen Cosgrove, Peter Coyote, Janet S. Crossen, Kim & David Daniels, Brian Komei Dempster, Matthew DeNichilo, Carl Dennis, Patrick Donnelly, Charles Douthat, Morgan Driscoll, Lynn Emanuel, Monica Ferrell, Elliot Figman, Laura Fjeld, Michael Foran, Jennifer Franklin, Sarah Freligh, Helen Fremont & Donna Thagard, Reginald Gibbons, Jean & Jay Glassman, Ginny Gordon, Lauri Grossman, Naomi Guttman & Jonathan Mead, Mark Halliday, Beth Harrison, Jeffrey Harrison, Page Hill Starzinger, Deming Holleran, Joan Houlihan, Thomas & Autumn Howard, Elizabeth Jackson, Christopher Johanson, Voki Kalfayan, Maeve Kinkead, David Lee, Jen Levitt, Howard Levy, Owen Lewis, Jennifer Litt, Sara London & Dean Albarelli, David Long, James Longenbach, Excelsior Love, Ralph & Mary Ann Lowen, Jacquelyn Malone, Donna Masini, Catherine McArthur, Nathan McClain, Richard McCormick, Victoria McCoy, Ellen McCulloch-Lovell, Judith McGrath, Debbie & Steve Modzelewski, Rajiv Mohabir, James T.F. Moore, Beth Morris, John Murillo & Nicole Sealey, Michael & Nancy Murphy, Maria Nazos, Kimberly Nunes, Bill O'Brien, Susan Okie & Walter Weiss, Rebecca Okrent, Sam Perkins, Megan Pinto, Kyle Potvin, Glen Pourciau, Kevin Prufer, Barbara Ras, Victoria Redel, Martha Rhodes, Paula Rhodes, Paula Ristuccia, George & Nancy Rosenfeld, M. L. Samios, Peter & Jill Schireson, Rob Schlegel & Martina Anderson, Roni & Richard Schotter, Jane Scovell, Andrew Seligsohn, James & Nancy Shalek, Soraya Shalforoosh, Peggy Shinner, Dara-Lyn Shrager, Joan Silber, Emily Sinclair, James Snyder & Krista Fragos, Alice St. Claire-Long,

Megan Staffel, Bonnie Stetson, Yerra Sugarman, Dorothy Tapper Goldman,
Marjorie & Lew Tesser, Earl Teteak, Parker & Phyllis Towle,
Pauline Uchmanowicz, Rosalynde Vas Dias, Connie Voisine, Valerie Wallace,
Doris Warriner, Ellen Doré Watson, Martha Webster & Robert Fuentes,
Calvin Wei, Bill Wenthe, Allison Benis White, Michelle Whittaker,
and Ira Zapin.